THE ANXIETY IN RELATIONSHIP CURE

A comprehensive guide on Why You Feel Anxious and How to Address The Problem From The Root

PHILIP RELATION

Table of Contents

Introduction

Anxiety affects nearly every facet of every relationship. When someone enters into a relationship, there have relatively simple expectations that go along with it. First and foremost, you assume the other person can fulfill the role of a partner. Being a partner involves the solid ability to communicate openly, offer companionship, contribute financially, hold on to a stable job, and eventually raise a family.

Communication is particularly important when it comes to romantic relationships. Being able to discuss all issues freely, make plans, and set goals for the future are all vital for a successful relationship. Otherwise, how could two partners handle their responsibilities, challenges, and expectations?

However, what happens if one of you is suffering from anxiety? Of course, it depends on how severe the anxiety is. However, no matter its level of development, a personal connection will be in some way affected. You or your partner might encounter difficulties in reacting in a healthy way when either of you expresses an opinion or an emotion. For instance, it is common to misread someone's intent or misinterpret the meaning of individual conversations. Anxiety works in many ways as a filter, and when it clouds your vision, you might act in a way that will eventually damage your relationship. Any joke, comment, or harmless critique can lead to an overreaction that will put a strain on any couple, even more than the anxiety itself.

If you find yourself in such a situation, you should take a break and see what warranted such a negative reaction or outburst. Your partner may be suffering from a form of anxiety, and they are overwhelmed by the strain. On the other hand, if you are the one with this problem, you need to acknowledge what's wrong and express it. If not, your partner will think you're cruel or aggressive for no reason, or that they are the problem.

Anxiety has a severe emotional effect on people, and the partner is always affected in some way as a result of seeing his or her significant other suffering and going through the whole life-crippling experience. And many cases in which the one suffering from anxiety will suppress any emotion or feeling. Emotions carry a great deal of power, and some people find it too challenging to face them. Those who are afraid to express themselves emotionally have likely lived in a household where the behavior was discouraged.

The act of suppressing emotions is a sign that the person is trying to hold on to a semblance of control. If you find yourself behaving this way, it might be because you are scared at the thought of losing that control and allowing the locked-up feelings to overwhelm you. Naturally, the biggest issue here is when it comes to negative emotions as they have such a substantial impact on a person's life. You might think that if you let it all out, you will change your partner's feelings.

And whatever good opinions and thoughts he or she has about you will be gone, and cause damage to the relationship. However, while you may think of this as a solution, it leads to even more problems. Acting this way will increase the amount of anxiety you experience. You will find less and less peace of mind until one day when it will all come out in a wild burst. It's difficult to suppress those feelings forever, and when they do come to the surface, the feeling will cloud all judgment.

Communication anxiety can also manifest itself without involving any emotional suppression. For instance, let's say your partner unloads only her most powerful feelings and emotions regularly. Some people cannot hold back on certain beliefs, so they lash out, and as a result, both of you end up feeling overwhelmed and confused, leading to another problem. Experiencing these outbursts often enough, you can start feeling that it's your job to find a solution to your partner's issues. It's not enough to notice the anxiety and the strain it's putting on your relationship. You get the feeling you are the sole savior of this partnership. Unfortunately, this usually makes things worse as your partner could start developing resentment towards you for their behavior.

Another communication problem is when you consider expressing yourself as a risky affair. Maybe you are wondering what will happen if you reveal what you honestly think. It is enough to trigger your anxiety as you are afraid of the uncertainty of the outcome. Frequently, this symptom stems from not having confidence in yourself and you are worried about an adverse reaction from your partner. In this case, you might be taking a great deal of time to rehearse what you will say and complicate things further by imagining all the possible scenarios.

Also, anxiety can have even worse repercussions if you or your partner will refuse to admit that you are suffering from it. Not acknowledging that there is a problem, especially one as grave as anxiety, will only lead to anger and irritable behavior that pushes the other person away. Running away from this problem often feels like it's an easier solution, especially by thinking that doing so will shelter the other person. Many people then act based on instinct and don't notice they're avoiding the problem or derailing the discussion by acting irritated. This defensive reaction is almost always caused by anxiety. They don't feel comfortable during the conversation, so they react without even thinking about their behavior, commonly leading to frustration and resentment for both parties.

With that said, now is the time for a little exercise, and you can ask yourself whether you or your partner are exhibiting signs of communication anxiety. The best approach to this little investigation is to take a journal and start making notes of any possible clues. Prepare several lists where you write down what kind of out-of-place signals you detect in a conversation. Don't just think about your partner, because you might be the problem without even realizing it. You should also take some time to reflect on how you react when you have a conversation with your partner. Think about his or her responses, as well. Finally, you can perform a mental exercise where you think about what you could've done to handle the conversation better. Make a list of situations where better communication would've prevented any feelings of resentment or anger between the two of you.

Social Situations

Being in certain social situations is difficult for many people who don't even suffer from any form of anxiety. However, those with anxiety will encounter other problems that wouldn't cross other people's minds. It's typical behavior to deny meal invitations from coworkers or friends, ignore unnecessary phone calls, and even avoid small family gatherings. While social situations are more specific and don't occur every day, there are also daily occurrences that can cause extreme amounts of anxiety. For instance, some have issues performing any task or responsibility as long as another human is being in their presence, looking over their shoulder.

Isolating yourself from any social situation usually leads to more than just personal social isolation. In some cases, this behavior can turn into a never-ending cycle of avoidance. The social aspects of life causing you anxiety, can, in turn, create even more tension in new situations. Avoidance reduces your ability to cope, and you will be dealing with even more fear during the next social gathering. This self-perpetuating cycle often leads to relationship problems, especially breakups, especially if one party is not suffering from any anxiety.

CHAPTER 1:

How to Help Your Anxious Partner and Yourself

Loving a Person with Anxiety

This part is dedicated to partners of people who struggle with anxiety. Relationships and love demand that we get involved in our partner's life and this means we always have to be supportive and loving. If you have a partner with one or more types of anxiety, you are already aware of how it can influence not just the relationship, but your life too. Anxiety comes in many forms, and there is no magic pill that can help. Anxiety is also an individual experience that can differ in many ways. The list of things we can do to help our partner when they are having an anxiety attack differs from person to person.

Acute Anxiety

Acute anxiety happens out of the blue. It can be caused by different things, certain situations, or other people you and your partner meet. It happens suddenly, and there is no time for planning and taking it slow. You need to be able to react at the moment and to know how to assess the situation. Understand what is happening, what your partner is going through, and come up with the right way that can help neutralize the anxiety. There are four steps you can take to be supportive and helpful in case of acute anxiety:

1. Be calm, be compassionate. If you are not, you won't be able to support your partner's needs at that moment. If you give in to anger, frustration, or anxiety, it won't help. It can even make things worse. You also need to remember not to give in to your partner's anxiety and accommodate it. In the long run, this is not helpful. Instead, offer understanding, not just solutions.
2. Assess your partner's anxiety. What level is it? What are the symptoms and signs of an anxiety attack? An anxiety attack can hit with a different strength each time. You need to be able to recognize it to choose actions appropriate to the given situation.
3. Remind your partner of the techniques that helped with anxiety attacks. Whether it is breathing or exercise, your partner is probably aware of their success in neutralizing anxiety. But in the given situation, maybe he or she needs reminding. Once they are on the right path to dealing with anxiety, your job is to provide positive reinforcement. Give praise and be empathetic once your partner executes techniques that will help with an anxiety attack.
4. Evaluate the situation. Is your partner's anxiety attack passing? If it is, be supportive and encourage your partner to continue whatever he is doing to lower his anxiety. If it stays at the same level, or increases, you should start the steps from the beginning and come up with different techniques and strategies to help your partner with an acute anxiety attack.

Chronic Anxiety

To address chronic anxiety, you might have to try out exposure therapy, as it is considered the golden standard of treatment by many people. Usually, it takes the guidance of a professional therapist to try exposure therapy. But, if the level of your partner's anxiety is not severe, you might feel comfortable enough to try it on your own. In this case, you have to act as a guide and learn how to be a supportive person for your partner.

You have to start with the least challenging situation and progress slowly and steadily towards more challenging ones. If anxiety isn't decreasing in the first challenge, it's not time to go to the second.

For example, let's say your partner has a fear of heights. He or she wants to overcome this fear and be able to climb the building's last floor. How will exposure therapy look in this case?

1. Tell your partner to look out the window from the ground floor for exactly one minute.
2. Climb to the second floor together with your partner. Remember that you are not just an exposure therapy guide; you also need to act as support. Make them look out the window from the second floor for one minute. In case of anxiety showing up in its first symptoms, remind your partner to do breathing exercises to lower its impact.
3. Once your partner feels better, they should try looking out the window again.

4. If no anxiety presents itself, you should leave your partner's side. They need to be able to look through the same window, but this time without you.
5. Climb to the third floor and repeat steps three and four. When your partner feels ready, continue to the fourth floor, sixth, and so on. If your partner's anxiety is too high, don't hesitate to stop. The first session doesn't need to take longer than 30 minutes.
6. Each new session needs to begin with the last comfortable floor your partner experienced. You don't need to always start from the ground floor, as your partner progresses, feeling no anxiety when looking through the window of the second, third, and even fourth floor.
7. Take time. Your partner will not be free of the fear in just a few days. Be patient and continue practicing exposure therapy in this way until your partner can achieve the goal and climb the last floor.
8. The goal of exposure therapy is not just to get rid of fear and anxiety. It should also teach your partner that he or she can control and tolerate discomfort. Your partner will have an opportunity to practice anxiety-reduction techniques in a safe and controlled environment, with you in the support role.

Specific Disorder Interventions

Under the guidance of a trained therapist, the two of you will learn how to approach it in the best possible way. Your partner's therapist might ask you to join in a few sessions, and he will teach you how to better help your partner in situations that elevate anxiety. If your partner is not diagnosed, but both of you suspect he might have a certain disorder, advise your partner to visit a doctor. Self-diagnosis can lead to mistakes, and you will make the wrong choices in how to approach your partner's anxiety.

Panic Disorder with Agoraphobia

If this is your partner's diagnosis, you two probably already have a pattern of behavior that is designed to accommodate your partner's anxiety. You probably follow your partner to social events, and you are the one who is in charge of running errands outside the house. This accommodation is counterproductive in the long run. You are showing that you care, love, and support your partner, but it prevents him or her from experiencing a full life. Your partner needs to learn how to overcome anxiety. You may approach a panic disorder with exposure therapy, so your partner becomes less dependent on you:

1. Choose an errand that your partner thinks he can handle himself. It can be shopping, going to a doctor's appointment alone, walking a dog, etc.
2. Plan what errands are more challenging for your partner and add them to the list. Write them down as *'To be accomplished in the future.'* It is important to work slowly but keep a clear vision of what needs to be accomplished.
3. Work together on slowly accomplishing the first task on your list. If it's going shopping alone, accompany your partner a few

times, so they are accustomed to the environment. When he or she feels confident enough to go alone, let them. Encourage and support their decision.

4. Once your partner accomplishes the task, be there to discuss his experience with it. Listen carefully and address any issues that might arise. Encourage your partner and keep track of his progress.

Obsessive-Compulsive Disorder

When it comes to OCD, what you can do for your partner is not to engage in his behaviors. Also, encourage him not to give in and repeat their compulsive behaviors. If you give in and comply with your partner's OCD, you will not be helping. Although it will surely elevate the tension made by your partner's OCD, complying will reinforce the fears. For example, if your partner asks you to go to the kitchen and make sure all appliances are off, you shouldn't comply. But you should also not argue or call your partner irrational. It is ineffective, and it will only deepen the anxiety.

Discuss with your partner how is it best to approach anxiety and agree on a strategy. This is where a professional therapist will be of most use to both of you. A professional can guide you through this conversation and help both of you feel comfortable discussing the delicate topic of your partner's disorder.

You will need to learn how to change from saying things like:

"I will not go to the kitchen again, you are imagining things, and being irrational" to "I appreciate your concern about the kitchen appliances, but we agreed that the best thing we can do is to help you learn how to manage the feelings you are having right now."

Your partner will agree for their benefit that the best thing you could do is stay by their side, not check the kitchen, and help them work through the anxiety. This can be done with breathing exercises that will help your partner calm down. In time, your partner will show less fear. The OCD will decrease, and you will feel less frustrated.

Generalized Anxiety Disorder

The behavior of people with GAD is similar to that of people who have OCD. They have fears about certain things, and these fears are not comforted by reassurance. GAD usually creates concerns that we all have. It can be about finances, health, and school. But people with GAD will blow these fears out of proportion and they will influence their daily life. If your partner is diagnosed with GAD, you are aware of how simple problems we face every day can sound like total catastrophes. Your partner probably assumes the worst possible end of certain situations.

It often happens that people with this affliction develop a constant feeling of inadequacy. They believe they are not good enough for their partners, and that they never will be. When this happens, they usually try to overcompensate and make everything perfect so their partner can love them. On the other hand, some may feel that there is nothing they can do and that there is no point in trying. They underperform reinforcing their feelings of inadequacy.

Social Phobia

Social phobia comes in many forms. It can make going to work a very difficult task, or it can make maintaining relationships impossible to achieve. A therapist uses this technique of testing the hypothesis of a patient. This is a very successful way of bringing realization to the patient that their fears and anxieties do not have a foundation. A therapist can teach a person with a social phobia the basic communication skills to prepare them for situations they might encounter in their endeavors to overcome anxiety.

CHAPTER 2:

Common Anxiety Disorders

So many people wonder how anxiety and depression are interconnected. Well, one thing that you need to understand is that when anxiety reaches a certain clinical level, it stops being just anxiety, but a disorder that could potentially result in depression. When anxiety persists for longer durations, the chances are that it will impair normal functioning. In other words, anxiety disorders become a habit that affects one's life seriously. It is important to note that anxiety must be diagnosed as early as possible. When it is better accounted for, it becomes very easy to control and treat. However, to avoid misdiagnosis, you must start first by ruling out hyperthyroidism, ADHD, or cocaine abuse, among others, that often share similar symptoms as an anxiety disorder.

That said, some common types of anxiety disorders include;

Generalized Anxiety

This is often anxiety that persists for too long and is characterized by extreme worry about something. For instance, one may worry too much about failing an exam, what happens if they were to die, or their inability to sleep, among others. What you will notice about people with generalized anxiety is that they are often described as being 'worried well.' Although it is often counterintuitive at the first glance, people with generalized anxiety often use their mental act of extreme worry to distract themselves temporarily from the emotions linked to what they are worried about in the first place.

Unfortunately, this extreme worry is what eventually results in excessive stress and anxiety.

Panic Disorder

When someone has panic attacks, this is often defined as having a sudden surge of extreme fear and anxiety that can get to optimal levels within minutes. This kind of fear is often characterized by symptoms associated with flight and fight responses. These symptoms include; an elevated heart rate, feeling light-headed, sweating, and chest tightness, among others. When you find yourself experiencing repeated panic attacks, then the chances are that you are persistently anxious about having those panic attacks or the results of panic attacks as the death of madness.

Specific Phobia

This is often referred to as anxiety that is specifically linked to something. For instance, you may be anxious about such things as flights, enclosed spaces, oceans, snakes, among others.

While true specific phobias are very rare, it is something that is commonly observed in people with panic disorders. In other words, you will find someone being irrationally afraid that a certain thing or situation could lead to panic and not that the specific situation or thing is dangerous in itself.

Social Anxiety

This is a condition in which one is fearful of social situations or gatherings. Typically, when one is exposed to real judgment or public scrutiny, they tend to coil up and freeze. This is often characterized by excessive worry and concerns about how others will evaluate or perceive them. In other words, they are worried about their public image/outlook.

Obsessive-Compulsive Disorder

This is a condition that is characterized by continued obsession, compulsion, or both. The thing with an obsession is that they are often thoughts, urges, or even images that keep recurring in an intrusive manner leading to distress and anxiety. For instance, you could be obsessing seeing your house on fire because you forgot to turn off the stove; however much you try to ignore or suppress the thought of it happening.

Compulsion, on the other hand, refers to recurring behaviors or rituals that one performs in an attempt to alleviate anxiety linked to their obsession. For instance, you could wash your hands as many times as possible before drying them, or you may count the number of steps in each building construction you get into, among others.

The thing with OCD is that people often focus on the intrusive mental activity and treat it as something dangerous or bad. This is mainly because they think that they are responsible for it or believe that it means something.

Post-Traumatic Stress Disorder (PTSD)

This often occurs when one is exposed to a real threat. This could be such threats as rape, murder, earthquakes, and floods, among others. Because of this exposure to in the past, they end up having recurring intrusive and distressing memories of their trauma. They may also try to avoid objects or certain situations that are linked to their trauma.

In other instances, people with PTSD often change their moods and thoughts associated with their trauma or may suffer increased arousal.

Think of PTSD as fear of memory. This is because one ends up having a fear of something that is in the surroundings that could trigger them to remember their traumatic events along with the sensations, thoughts, or feelings of the trauma. Because of this, they tend to get pre-occupied with avoiding anything that could trigger their trauma. The worst thing is that this attempt to avoid it often leads to depression, isolation, and substance abuse. It also is associated with increased levels of anxiety.

Separation Anxiety

This is age-inappropriate distress that is linked with separation from someone, a person viewed as an attachment figure. In most cases, this often refers to a parent. This explains why it is typically observed in childhood with children refusing to go to school. However, this has also been seen in adulthood. For instance, a spouse may suffer separation anxiety when their partner leaves town for business meetings.

How Does Anxiety Work?

However, the next most important thing is for us to discuss why it happens at all. Why is that that one can get irrationally afraid of something and then stay afraid?

This brings us to how anxiety works in the first place and how can we leverage this knowledge to benefit us.

Well, one important thing that you need to bear in mind at all times is that the only important concept as far as anxiety is concerned is avoidance. To be more specific, the main reason why so many people experience persistence in the clinical levels of anxiety is that they try hard to avoid their anxiety.

While this may sound counterintuitive at first, one thing that you must understand is that at the core, every anxiety disorder is the same. Although they may look and feel different for some reason, they share similar dynamics. This means that people with anxiety disorders often have learned to train their minds to be afraid of their sensations, thoughts, and emotions. And all that has been done by accident.

It is interesting to note that the very thing that they try in an attempt to make their anxiety better is avoiding it altogether. This is exactly what makes it even worse! To understand how it works, it is critical that we start with the little chunks of neurons located at the center of the brain, referred to as the amygdala.

Your Amygdala

The main role of this part of the brain is to ensure that you are safe from danger or other forms of physical threat. It is the part of the brain that helps you stay alive. To achieve this, the amygdala tells you to look out for any potential threat. This explains why you keep scanning your surroundings for any suspicious object or event.

If it finds something that it perceives as a threat, it sounds an alarm that tells the body to get ready to deal with the threat. It does this by stimulating the secretion of adrenaline and activating the fight and flight response. This is when you start experiencing faster breathing rates, muscle tension, increased blood pressure, and supply to the head and the torso, and other body extremities for efficient delivery of oxygen in readiness for fight or flight.

Well, all this is superb if a real physical threat is confronting you, like someone holding a gun to your head in a dark alley or a venomous snake jumps and coils around your body. In such situations, your hope would be for that amygdala to stimulate as much adrenaline as possible to help you get out safe and sound.

However, this comes in when the amygdala is confused about what is a real threat to your survival and what is not. Is it worthy of stimulating full-blown adrenaline for a fight-or-flight response, or is it something not worth it at all because they are not a threat to your survival?

To illustrate this, let us consider an example.

How Avoidance Contributes To Fear Learning and Increased Anxiety

We would all agree that hiking is not all that dangerous an activity, right? While there are risks that are associated with hiking, such as falling off a cliff or being attacked by wild and dangerous animals, the truth is that in most cases, hiking is a very safe outdoor activity.

What is interesting is that so many people are very anxious about going out for a hike, but choose to turn down an invitation to go hiking irrespective of who is asking them. They choose to go for walks in paths that they are well versed with and try as much as they can to avoid hiking by all means possible, including watching movies about hiking and nature trails.

You may be thinking, "But how is that possible? How can she/he be afraid of hiking when it is one of the perfectly safe activities?"

Well, one thing you need to understand is that the issue does not lie in what they believe. Instead, what matters most is what the amygdala tells them to believe. In most cases, the amygdala will strongly believe in the things we teach them.

According to research, it is evident that people with anxiety have likely triggered a process referred to as Fear Learning. This process has, in turn, taught their amygdala to be extremely sensitive to anything that could be potentially dangerous and afraid of things that may not be a threat in the first place.

To better understand this concept, consider yourself an average Joe going out for a hike in the foothills. After half-an-hour, you see something dark and curly on the trails. Immediately, the amygdala fires up, and you become alert to a potentially venomous snake. Your heart starts beating fast, muscles tense up, your heart rate is elevated, and you start to sweat.

But, what is most important as far as anxiety is concerned is the step you take after that. While the amygdala alerts you to scan your surroundings for threats and stimulates the release of adrenaline in readiness for flight or fight, what you need to bear in mind is that this part of the brain has an error correction mechanism. This mechanism is what allows you to verify whether the flag raised is correct. It also goes a long way in gauging how you respond to the potential threat. It uses that behavior to confirm or deny the initial threat evaluation.

CHAPTER 3:

How to Talk to a New Partner About Your Anxiety

Being involved with somebody with issues of uneasiness can be horrendously upsetting. Once in a while, it can seem as though dread, somebody who wobbles among you and your companion, is a third individual in the relationship. This individual consistently plants questions and vulnerability.

In any case, there is no requirement for nervousness to demolish the relationship or to make it hard to appreciate. As a matter of fact, you can adore each other all the more profoundly by understanding apprehension all in all and how it influences both your accomplice and your relationship. Instruction can likewise diminish a lot of pressure.

The book separates all you have to learn and do when somebody is restless to discuss: how to support your accomplice, how uneasiness can affect your relationship, looking for your emotional well-being and that's only the tip of the iceberg. Continue perusing if you need to guarantee that your organization doesn't turn into a third individual.

Nervousness Filled Conversation

If you ask or conclude it after monthly gatherings, there will be a moment that your accomplice uncovers that they need to manage dread. It is a crucial time in the relationship, along these lines be touchy and don't pass judgment. He will be much obliged to you for confiding in you with this information, which you presumably didn't impart to numerous individuals. Consider it to be the beginning of a discussion that you can regularly reemerge.

Getting Anxiety and Knowing What It is doing to Your Partner

Learning dread and what your accomplice is doing will assist you with understanding and help them collaborate with some fundamental realities about uneasiness. Clinician Dave Carbonell, Ph.D. therapist Dr. Helen Odessky, among others, recommended remembering these:

- Anxiety is typical. Everyone has it. It turns into an issue or turmoil just if that it is not kidding.
- Anxiety is a genuine issue, not a composite. It's an issue in psychological well-being.
- Anxiety can be a devastating condition that keeps individuals from working and carrying on with an ordinary life.
- Anxiety makes individuals experience flight and fights reactions and stress over dangerous issues, including whether an accomplice may cheat or leave.
- You can't "fix" anxiety.

- Many individuals who have nervousness issue wish they never had it. They are worried that their uneasiness is a weight for other people.
- Many individuals have incredible connections and are cheerful regardless of managing uneasiness.
- Symptoms of uneasiness, reliably or both may happen in waves. Individuals with a nervousness issue or issues can have timeframes when they have no side effects.
- Anxiety isn't balanced or legitimate. This makes the individuals stress over something even when there is no proof or when it does not merit stress. It likewise makes them act nonsensically in some cases. Your accomplice presumably realizes that.
- Anxiety isn't a shortcoming.
- Anxiety can be dealt with. Psychotherapy can reduce manifestations and show individuals how to treat them better.

A great many people have a portion of these stressing considerations in any event. They are a typical piece of a relationship, especially another one.

Be that as it may, individuals with nervousness issues or an uneasiness issue will in general have this tension many times and all the more seriously.

"Our musings are dominating and heading straight into the direst outcome imaginable," said Michelene Wasil, a specialist who comprehends both individual and mental tension.

Uneasiness causes physiological impacts, including brevity of breath, restlessness, and tension. On edge, individuals can respond to worry with the battle or flight reaction, as though stress were a physical assault.

In some cases, troubling musings persuade your accomplice to act in manners that pressure and stress the relationship. For instance, therapist Jennifer B. Rhodes stated, individuals with tension frequently check their accomplice's association with unbound methodologies. These procedures for the most part address one of their on-edge feelings.

Let us state that your accomplice is on edge to be the first to start correspondence. You don't care for him as much as he needs you to, he starts to stress since you don't send the primary content as frequently as he does. Nervousness strengthens and he begins to feel that if he didn't connect first, you would never converse with him.

He concurs that it's a smart thought to fantasize about you some time to fix this dread. This powers you to convey first. Maybe a few times you'll contact him before he feels great, realizing you'd put forth the attempt. The confirmation urges him to question his absurd and apprehensive conviction that you won't hit first. However, it's unmistakably not a decent methodology.

Tragically, there are numerous practices of seeing someone persuaded by tension. Here are a couple of more models:

- Being controlling
- Perfectionism

- Passive forceful conduct or being avoidant
- Being excessively basic
- Being bad-tempered and furious
- Having trouble centering and being occupied

If you are involved with somebody with social tension issues, the nervousness is probably going to influence your public activity, forestalling, or showing hostile conduct. Perfectionism is meeting someone with social uneasiness. You will be unable to carry your accomplice to all the get-togethers or gatherings you need to join in. Like different sorts of tension, this may offer ascent to contradictions or prompt both of you to become separated.

CHAPTER 4:

Causes of Anxiety

Different unreasonable practices emerge because of tension in a relationship. Some of them as referenced before incorporate pulling back from the relationship, acting unapproachable, remaining protected, etc. As we think about our past, we promptly acknowledge there is an assortment of impacts in our past affecting our present life and choices. The connection designs obvious in our grown-up life have their foundations followed back to our youthful ages. The data passed by the pundit inward voice and the mental protections we apply are because of the assortment of life encounters.

Tuning in to the negative inward voice can make us to:

1. Become Tenacious

In specific situations, nervousness emotions can make us act urgent and bug our accomplices. Nervousness can make an individual quit feeling as free and solid as he/she did before getting into the relationship. Therefore, he/she may discover him/herself self-destructing effectively, acting unreliable, getting desirous, or staying away from those exercises that require autonomy.

2. Control

Our human instinct requests that when we feel compromised, we endeavor to control or rule the circumstance. If we feel undermined in a relationship, odds are, we will attempt to recover control of the circumstance. What we neglect to acknowledge is that the sentiments of danger are not genuine; rather, they are because of the inward basic voice that is contorting reality.

When taking control, we may begin setting rules on what an accomplice ought to and ought not to do, who to visit, converse with, connect with, and whatnot. This is a frantic endeavor to ease our sentiments of uneasiness and instability. This controlling conduct can raise hatred and distance our accomplices.

3. Reject

If that a relationship is causing us to feel stressed, a typical and out of line protection instrument is dismissal. We begin to act standoffish, that is, unapproachable. We become some way or another segregated and cold. This guarantees if the accomplice out of nowhere leaves, we won't feel torment. At the end of the day, we are securing ourselves by getting the best of our accomplices. These activities of dismissal can either be inconspicuous or obvious. In any case, they are a certain method of making a separation between two accomplices by working up uncertainty.

4. Retain

Now and again, rather than unequivocally dismissing our accomplices in light of tension, a few people will, in general, retain from them. For example, when things have gotten extremely cross and an individual feels worked up, he/she withdraws. Individuals who use retaining strategies to manage tension in a relationship keep down either a piece of their fondness of an entire portion of the relationship through and through. Retaining may appear to be innocuous since the accomplice isn't confronting dismissal of tenacity and control, however, note; it is one of the gentlest and calmest enemies of fascination and enthusiasm in a relationship.

5. Retreat

Tension prompts dread and fearing a relationship you are in can be truly pushing. To keep away from such pressure, countless individuals decide to withdraw, that is, abandoning the genuine demonstrations of affection and supplanting it with a dream bond. By definition, a dream bond is a bogus deception that replaces genuine emotions and demonstrations of affection. In this condition of imagination, an individual spotlights the structure rather than substance. He/she abandons the genuine and imperative piece of the relationship and remains in it to have a sense of security. In a dream bond, individuals take part in numerous dangerous practices, for example, retaining or participating in non-indispensable exercises. The subsequent separation prompts the finish of a relationship. As much as the retreat will shield you from sentiments of dread, it will give you a misguided feeling of wellbeing and you will lose a great deal of valuable time living in a dream. What a great many people neglect to acknowledge is that by the day's end, they should confront reality.

Love is a delightful thing, however, believe it or not, it has its requests and results. Truly, love is an exceptionally confounded thing. Why so? Since, while we are occupied with searching for it (Because it is a delightful thing), we additionally realize that it is one of the fundamental drivers of misery on the planet. We don't know about a thing that can make an individual urgent how love does. Love is our primary purpose behind living and a significant due to torment in our lives. It is the main feeling that can divert anybody over the world from being a sort and delicate individual to a harsh and angry person. Also, it couldn't care less about status, sex, or age.

Strikingly, as individuals search for this two-fold edged blade called love, they likewise experience something different; Relationship tension. We as a whole encounter uneasiness seeing someone either quietly or strongly. It is entirely expected to be on edge about things, particularly love. Be that as it may, for this situation, we are concentrating on the sort of nervousness that shakes the establishment of a relationship so hard that it breaks. This sort of tension makes an individual uncertainty of love. Relationship tension is apparent when two individuals invest a large portion of their energy being restless about the relationship and agonizing over it as opposed to tending to it strongly.

Anyway, if that it isn't unexpected to have worries about a relationship, how might one tell that he/she is encountering relationship uneasiness? The following are a few signs that one can search for showing that one is having extraordinary or pointless relationship uneasiness.

A. Over-investigating

This is the inclination to overthink things, and even actually search for shortcomings or negative angles. There is a satiating that goes, over-investigation causes loss of motion. Here is the thing; there is nothing amiss with utilizing rationale. Indeed, it is alright to be basic or suspicious in any event until you make sense of things. The capacity to consider things completely before tolerating them can assist you in telling the difference between fiction and reality: what is a negligible dream and what is the truth.

Be that as it may, there is a drawback to over-analyzing a relationship. You will never be happy with the appropriate response. Everything that is said or done is dependent upon investigation and increasingly questioning. A genuine case of over-investigation and its results is the point at which an individual starts to overthink things and therefore makes situations in his/her brain, thus putting together their activities concerning nonexistent occasions that have not occurred at this point.

Picture this; you are on a first or second date. Your garments, shoes, and language give a decent early introduction. Everything about the imminent relationship looks brilliant. Be that as it may, when the accomplice shows up, you begin bombarding them with a gazillion inquiries regarding their previous connections. "Have you been in another relationship? What number of ex's do you have? For what reason did you leave them? Was there conning included? Who started the separation? Are your folks still together? Do they have a decent relationship?"

Perhaps you have been to a date where the other individual was asking you these sorts of inquiries. Do you realize why individuals do this? It is because they are searching for security. They would prefer not to come up short but then they are exceptionally terrified of allowing everything just to be as it is. It is more about security than affection. "Is this individual liable to say a final farewell to me?"

On the more brilliant side, it is thoroughly fine for an individual to communicate his/her stresses over affection and being harmed. In any case, it is completely off-base to pose an individual a few inquiries that are excessively close to home for the sake of ensuring yourself. It isn't right on all levels to constrain somebody to review a few things that may be difficult for them. Try not to ask individuals inquiries that cause the individual to feel cross-examined. Also, if you find that you can't prevent yourself from posing these inquiries, it may demonstrate that you are experiencing relationship uneasiness. You can't control your feelings of trepidation about connections and responsibilities, accordingly, searching for approaches to approve your reasons.

B. Dread of Being in a Genuine Relationship

To what extent would two individuals be able to take before choosing to be in a genuine relationship? To what extent can individuals know each other before consenting to take things to the following level? There is no particular duration. Everything relies upon the individuals in question and how well they know one another. Some take three dates, others one month while others may take a very long time before being prepared.

If that an individual has relationship nervousness, his/her response to each demand for duty will be "Never" or "I am not prepared." Regardless of whether the individual is infatuated or not, he/she won't focus on the relationship. The genuine purpose behind this absence of duty is the profound situated dread at the rear of the person's brain. This individual is worried about the possibility that he/she is going to wind up alone, once more. Along these lines, he/she stays away from those circumstances that may set him/her up for double-crossing.

Experiencing passionate feelings includes confronting genuine dangers. It is tied in with permitting yourself to feel powerless. The crucial step of adoration is setting a monstrous measure of trust in another person and permitting him/her to form our hearts. You can't be 100% sure that the individual will deal with you. You are not yet sure if the individual is the one for you. Thus, nervousness will make you think "If that I am not 100 percent secure with this individual, is there a need for reality?" Then excusing somewhat more, you will find a solution like, "If you don't get submitted, you won't get injured." Now, that is a thought brought to you by tension.

All things considered, this is what's going on; you are feeling apprehensive in this manner, hesitant to focus on an individual. Subsequently, you will never learn through understanding. If that you are continually dismissing the odds of adoration. In what manner will you know the genuine article that may assist you in managing the relationship's uneasiness?

C. You Have a Terrible Temper

The most terrible thing about relationship tension is that it influences the two individuals in a relationship. Indeed, it harms you and your accomplice, unjustifiably.

CHAPTER 5:

How Does It Affect Actions and Thoughts?

When one person in a relationship suffers from anxiety, this can have a lot of negative effects. This is especially true if the one who suffers from the disorder doesn't get understanding or support from their partner. Since anxiety involves fear, stress, and excessive worrying, these may develop into irrational thoughts. In turn, these thoughts can have an impact on how your partner perceives you and your relationship.

Because of your partner's disorder, you need to work extra hard to maintain your relationship through avoidance, dependence, and other challenges. Even if your partner starts sabotaging your relationship, you should try to understand why they are doing it while helping them overcome their insecurities and negativities. When it comes to helping a partner with anxiety, focus on understanding, support, and love. All of these things can help you weather any storm to keep your relationship intact. Of course, this journey is easier said than done. Sometimes, even if you know what to do from what you learn within these pages, taking action when faced with real-life situations can be very difficult, especially when negative feelings emerge within you. Therefore, you should learn how anxiety may affect your relationship so that you are prepared for what may come. This will help lessen the impact, thus allowing you to think and respond more appropriately.

How Can Anxiety Affect Your Relationship?

If you have ever been extremely anxious about something in the past, then you know how debilitating this feeling can be. Now try to imagine how your partner feels when anxiety comes knocking, but this time, it doesn't go away. This means that your partner would be in a constant state of fear, worry, and anxiety. Unless your partner does something to deal with these feelings or you do something to help them, they might start taking a toll on your relationship. Anxiety is truly a debilitating condition, not just for those who suffer from these symptoms, but for those who love them, too. Here are some ways anxiety can affect your relationship:

Anxiety May Break Down Your Connection and Your Trust

Relationships are built on trust and as time goes by, this trust builds an unbreakable connection filled with love. However, when one of you, in this case, your partner, develops anxiety, it will start eating away at the trust you have worked so hard to build. When this happens, your connection may break down, as well. As your partner battles with their anxiety, they will feel differently about you and your relationship.

If you don't notice what is happening with your partner, their condition may get worse. Then, your partner will feel ashamed or even afraid of their anxiety which, in turn, may cause them to pull away from you. Your partner might start doubting how you feel about them, how much they mean to you, and even whether you still love them. When your partner surrenders to these doubts, they might also lose their trust in you.

Anxiety Might Cause Your Partner to Reject You

The opposite of anxiety is acceptance, therefore, if your partner suffers from an anxiety disorder, they might reject you. Of course, this would be very painful, even if you know that your partner's disorder is the major cause of their rejection. In such a case, try to hang on and continue helping your partner. Giving up or accepting their rejection will just bring your relationship to an end.

As you can see, anxiety can wreak havoc on your relationship. This is why you must help each other so that you can defeat the disorder instead of allowing it to defeat you. One of the most important ways to do this is by communicating.

Anxiety Might Take the Joy Out of Your Relationship

If all the other effects above happen in your relationship, you both might end up unhappy. Think about it: if your partner behaves irrationally and you react by arguing with them or losing patience, how can joy remain a part of your relationship? Sadly, this is a common thing that may happen, especially if you don't work with your partner to help them manage their disorder.

Anxiety May Cause Your Partner to Become Avoidant

While some people become too dependent on those around them, especially their partners, others cope through avoidance. To deal with their feelings, your partner might start avoiding you and the other people around them. You may notice your partner becoming distant, aloof, or even cold. In some cases, they might even become emotionally unavailable. Even if you had a strong relationship in the past, anxiety can destroy this by causing your partner to become avoidant.

Anxiety May Cause Your Partner to Procrastinate and Panic

An anxious person may feel worried or fearful of the surrounding people. Because of this, they might think that they need to hide their true self. If your partner's anxiety causes them to feel this way, you might see a different side of them emerging. Since your partner doesn't feel like they can be themselves with you, they start panicking and procrastinating. This is when you might see them avoiding chores, making excuses, coming up with distractions, and doing other things that aren't like your partner at all.

Anxiety Might Make Your Partner Overly Dependent On You

Sometimes, people who suffer from anxiety might yearn for an intense closeness with their partner all the time. The reason for this yearning is to seek regular feelings of reassurance or support from their partner. Unfortunately, when you have a partner who is overly dependent on you, you might not be able to separate yourself from them. Even if you convince your partner to spend some time apart (like if you need to travel for business or you want to go out with your friends), your partner might end up overthinking. They might begin catastrophizing about worst-case scenarios, and when you finally get home, they start an argument with you. If this keeps happening, it will affect your relationship.

Anxiety May Cause Your Partner to Behave Selfishly

Anxiety often causes people to act irrationally. If your partner becomes overly fearful, they might only focus on their problems or concerns. Everything will become about them, and this causes them to act only for their benefit. To you, these actions will seem selfish, especially when your partner doesn't seem to even consider your thoughts or feelings. But they are only doing this as they try to deal with or overcome their anxiety.

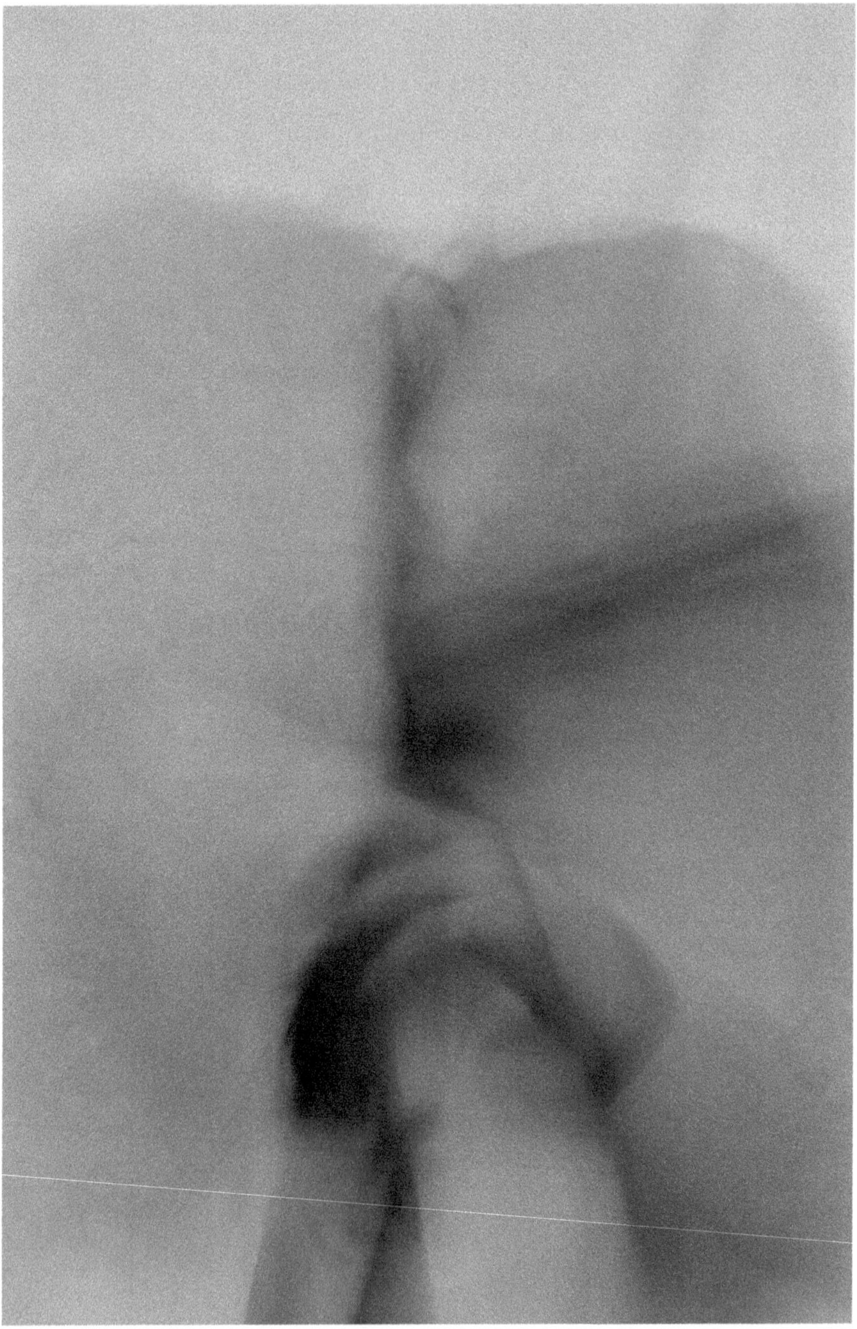

CHAPTER 6:

How Excessive Attachment and Jealousy Hinders the Well Being Of the Couple

Jealousy can unfortunately ruin even the best relationships. It can be a powerful signal that it is time for you to change or risk losing an otherwise fulfilling relationship. Jealousy can be a good checklist to better understand your underlying feelings, taking immediate action, and protect your relationship from experiencing the disastrous fallout of your jealous thoughts or behavior. Here are some of the most foolproof techniques to help you tackle jealousy and insecurity in relationships with ease.

Question Yourself Each Time

Each time you find yourself feeling even remotely jealous, question the underlying feeling behind the complex emotion of jealousy. Is jealousy a consequence of my anger, anxiety, or fear? What is it about this situation that makes me jealous? When you question you're jealously critically, you are a few steps away from taking constructive steps to convert a cloud of negativity into a bundle of positivity.

Be Open About Your Insecurities

Discussing your insecurities with your partner will help you create a frank and open communication channel. Rather than doing and saying crazy things to your partner, be upfront, and share your feelings. Say something similar to "I apologize for bothering you regarding your friendship with ABC, but it is not my lack of trust in you. I simply feel insecure about it."

Admitting it is you and not the other person who goes a long way in resolving your relationship issues over hurling accusations at your partner. Together, you can work better on your insecurities if you both acknowledge it and take active steps to eliminate it.

Learn to Trust People

Learn to get into the habit of trusting people more. Choose a trusting disposition over a distrustful attitude. Unless you have concrete evidence about someone, take their word for it. Going around snooping, stalking your partner, and behaving like a suspicious maniac only harms your relationship further. Rather, if there is no reason to be suspicious other than a feeling of insecurity or jealously, let it go.

Get to the Root of Your Feelings

It can be hard to objectively assess why you feel pangs of jealously every time someone compliments your partner, or he/she speaks warmly with his/her colleagues. It can be highly tempting to blame another person for your emotions. However, getting to the root of your jealousy by being more self-aware is the foundation to free yourself from its shackles. Take a more compassionate and objective look at the origination of your jealousy. Think about the potential causes of feelings of insecurity.

For instance, if you find yourself being increasingly jealous of your partner; know why you feel it. Is it because you don't want to lose him/her? Is it because your relationship ended due to a similar reason? Do you suffer from a false sense of self-entitlement that your partner's time belongs only to you? Do you feel what you feel because of a sense of inadequacy that constantly makes you think "you aren't good enough?" Once you identify the underlying reasons causing feelings of jealousy and insecurity, it becomes easier to deal with your behavior.

Write Down Your Deepest Thoughts

Journaling is known to be one of the most effective techniques for bringing to the forefront your deepest feelings and emotions. It helps you discover multiple layers of your personality to achieve greater self-awareness. For instance, you may constantly harbor feelings of insecurity because you were raised by neglectful parents or you may never feel you are "good enough" because you were raised by parents who had extremely high and unreasonable expectations of you.

People who have been neglected in their childhood often feel they aren't worthy enough to be loved. This, in turn, causes them to think that their partner is seeking someone more worthy or deserving of love than them, which creates feelings of insecurity. Writing down may help you discover certain events, circumstances, and facets which may directly be responsible for your irrational behavior. Once you've nailed down underlying feelings behind the jealousy, it is way simpler to manage it.

Learn From Your Jealousy

Jealousy can be converted into learning or inspiration if you channelize it productively. For instance, if your partner plays the guitar well and finds himself/herself the cynosure of all eyes at a party, you can up your skills, too, by learning from him/her or signing up for guitar lessons. Instead of wallowing in defeatist self-pity, you have transformed your negative feelings into something positive.

Jealousy Doesn't Mean Something Will Happen

We need to understand that our jealous hunches do not necessarily mean the act is occurring. Just because we fear something is going to happen doesn't mean it will happen. A majority of the time, our fears are unfounded and not even remotely close to coming true. Just because your partner is somewhere else, and you fear he/she is with someone else, doesn't mean he/she is proposing marriage on a date. Understand the difference between thoughts and actual events. The make-believe imaginations of our destructive minds are often far from reality. Paranoia or replaying a worst-case scenario is common among people suffering from jealousy or insecurity. They imagine things that have no basis in reality. For instance, your partner may call or visit an ex to express his/her condolences when the ex's mother passes away. This doesn't in any way imply that your partner is still hooked to the ex.

However, you may find yourself imagining terrible things that may be the result of sheer jealousy and paranoia. Rather than imagining negative things, try shifting the focus of how wonderful your partner is to be considerate and pleasant with an ex. This might be the very reason that made you fall in love with him/her. See what you did there? You shifted your feelings from insecurity to pride, from untrue suspicions to a positive reality.

Get Rid of Past Relationship Garbage

A strong reason why you are always paranoid about your current partner cheating on you can be traced back to an earlier relationship. You may have had an ex-partner cheat on you with your best friend. The betrayal may have had such a severe impact that you view every relationship in a similar distrustful light.

However, understand that your current partner has nothing to do with your relationship. He/she should not have to bear the brunt of what someone else did. Painting everyone with the same brush can be a disastrous mistake in any relationship. There is a solid reason your earlier relationship did not last, and you should leave the baggage of your earlier relationship where it belongs–in the trash can.

Focus Your Energies Elsewhere

Rather than obsessing over who your partner is cheating you with, try to develop interests outside of your relationship.

Do not make it the nucleus of your existence even if it means a lot to you. Pursue your hobbies, be a part of local clubs, volunteer for good causes, be active in the local community, play a sport, learn different languages, take fun dance/aerobics sessions, be a part of a local book club–anything that shifts your focus from overwhelming jealous thoughts to productive channelization of energy.

Surround Yourself with Meaningful Relationships

People are often so wrapped up in their romantic relationship that there is a tendency to distance ourselves from all other relationships. We believe in spending every waking minute of our lives with our partners. This only leads to a greater feeling of fear and insecurity because we realize that once this relationship ceases to exist, we have no other meaningful relationship as our safety net. We tend to develop greater feelings of insecurity and jealousy when we have no one to fall back on.

It helps to not make a single relationship in the center of your universe and develop several meaningful friendships. Do no distance from your close friends after getting into a relationship. Talk to them, spend time with them, do fun things together (that you probably did in school or college), have lunch dates, travel with them, and more. This will give you a life outside of your and your partner's time together. Once you have a momentous life outside your relationship, you will be less likely to wallow in self-pity and self-induced sulks. You will always have someone to talk to if you are surrounded by family or friends who understand and love you unconditionally.

Mindfulness for Managing Your Emotions

Mindfulness is a great way to calm your nerves and manage runaway emotions. Tune into your physical and mental self by identifying your feelings, thoughts, and emotions by taking deep breaths. Try to detach yourself from overpowering negative emotions such as jealousy and insecurity. Every time you find yourself overcome with thoughts of jealousy or insecurity, practice mindful meditation.

Find a quiet corner that is free from distraction, sit in a comfortable position, and clear your mind by eliminating all thoughts and take deep breaths. Focus only on the present and your deep breathing without allowing your mind to wander. If you find your mind drifting, gently bring it back to the present by concentrating on your bodily sensations. Daily meditation sessions can help you break free from ugly thoughts and behavior patterns.

Do Not Judge Others Based on Your Past Actions

Ever notice how suspicious people are always suspicious of others? Or how liars think everyone around them is lying? Our perceptions of people and their motives are often a reflection of who we are. Stop using your past or present behavior as a yardstick for perceiving your partner's actions. For instance, if you have a history of being involved with married men/women, do not assume that no married man/woman can ever be trusted and start mistrusting your spouse. Just because you did or are doing something does not mean he/she is indulging in it, too. People who often have loyalty issues themselves constantly attack their partners for being unfaithful or immoral. There is a greater need to shift the blame from their inability to cope with issues related to unfaithfulness. Acknowledge that there is a problem, talk to a therapist about it and try to treat it rather than making your partner bear the brunt of your follies. Sometimes people fail to understand why despite giving their partner no reason to feel insecure or ever being unfaithful to them they are still made to feel like lying scums. The problem often lies with the person suspecting them and not the person at the receiving end of these unfortunate suspicions.

Avoid Being a Victim of Relationship Games

People often try to feel great about themselves by purportedly getting their partner to feel jealous. Do not fall into the trap. Displaying any signs of jealousy will only encourage your partner's behavior. Tell your partner firmly that indulging in a jealousy/insecurity inducing behavior only demeans him/her and won't make him/her feel any better about himself/herself. Even if you feel jealous, try to keep a stoic and unaffected demeanor, which should eventually stop these excruciatingly uncomfortable, attention-drawing tactics.

CHAPTER 7:

Techniques for Eliminating Stress

Each person deals with stress in their own way. This is not to say that these are voluntary reactions. These are *in*voluntary responses our bodies make to compensate for the effects of the causes of factors of the stress. Our bodies respond to the effects of stress differently. Some people may experience shortness of breath and exhibit trembling and tremors. Others may exhibit stress physically, getting stomach aches, headaches or they may get sick frequently. It is impossible to eliminate stress given the demands of your life, the society we live in, your job, your relationship, and of course, yourselves.

With stress being a part of most societies, with a set of different commonalities and variances, making it a point to identify individual and specific stressors, can allow the individual to take back some control by employing stress management techniques to lessen the stress effects on one's overall health. Knowing what demands the most of your energy, identifying what depletes you of the energies your body needs to function optimally, is one manner how you can overcome the negativity brought about by those situations. Read about some ways one can help cope with stress below.

Taking care of your health is vital to not only your physical health but your mental stability as well. Taking care of your health means that you will need to be mindful of what you eat. Sticking to a balanced diet is not only beneficial to the body but the mental balance as well and is a healthy step towards combating stressful situations. When an individual exercises regularly, even if it is just a quick 30-minute brisk walk around the block or a regular bike ride to work, it is invaluable. Getting a proper and moderate workout for your health is essential to curbing the effects of stress. Having the proper amount of sleep at the correct time is a catalyst for a clear head. A good night's rest allows for better decision making.

Sometimes, a good ear is all you need to blow off some steam and avoid further stress from progressing and worsening. Support is usually found from friends and or family by talking about the source of the demands on your person. It is easy to isolate oneself under stressful situations or when going through a difficult spell, avoid staying away from being around the company which may lead to more serious mental issues like depression and suicide.

Learn to remove yourself from a stressful situation. Sometimes, stepping away from the situation which causes you stress can help you clear your head of the cause of your anxiety. Taking the high road can also mean turning away from the situation that causes you stress. It is also good to be reminded that using drugs and alcohol as means of escaping the realities of a stressful event may help on a short-term basis but can cause bigger and worse problems in the long run. The ill-effects of the use of illegal drugs, self-medication, and excessive alcohol consumption during stressful events in one's life leads to dependency on substances that first does not help us in facing the situation, thereby learning how to make decisions on future responses.

Every person is bound to deal with stress in one way or another simply because stress is a part of life. What we need to keep in mind is that not all stress is bad because it does give us the ability to assess a situation and make calculated deductions about the best response to any given situation. Concern does creep in when stress is prolonged because of the impact it has on our overall health.

With more than a host of stressful situations waiting around the bend with each day we traverse, it is more than ever important to accept the stressors that can trigger off stress hormones. From minor everyday incidents that come along with the birth of each day to the more long-lasting, more chronic forms of stress that are less prioritized of our everyday lives tucked away and not dealt with by us. Proactively finding ways for you to deal with the underlying, tucked away stressors in your life will empower you to better deal with the everyday challenges. To manage stress means to maintain a fulfilling and healthy life.

If we could see that there are thoughts that are creating more stress and not our situation we would be better able to manage stress. Being able to recognize this is good news to you because then you would be equipped with the right skill set to recognize fact from supposed thoughts in your current situation. Keep in mind that you don’t have to change your situation to be stress-free, you just have to change the way you think about the situation.

To be free of what is creating stress, we first need to identify what specific thoughts, stories, or beliefs spawn the stress. Do this whenever you feel stressed. Ask yourself an honest question: "What outcome am I afraid of?"

For example, let's say you have a report that you need to submit to your boss and you worry about whether the report is accurate good enough, and acceptable to your boss or perhaps you might be going out on a date you and you might be worried that the person you are going out with will not like you or perhaps you are preparing for an exam and you are worried that you might fail this test.

The next question to ask yourself after you've determined to answer for the first is what outcome I think is the best. Your answers may be, "It would be best if I prepare the report we had of time and check that everything is in order." And perhaps for your date, you might say, "I'll just be myself and see where it goes from there," and for the exam, you might give yourself an answer like "I need to learn to study more efficiently." When you determine the best outcome, you set yourself up to succeed. How you may ask is this? Asking yourself what the best outcome is allows you to better prepare yourself. You are essentially avoiding the worst possible outcome to be free from your thoughts to be free from that specific stress.

Once you understand that your thoughts are creating your stress and want to identify the specific stress, the next thing you have to do is not believe that thought. This sounds like a radical and difficult step to manage the stress, but it is your way of helping yourself to eliminate unnecessary, unmerited, and stressful thoughts.

When a person believes words to be true, there is a corresponding emotion that goes along with the words you hear or think. Notice that, on the other hand, when you don't believe that there's any truth to the words you hear, no emotions are involved. Asking these questions and giving real, honest answers yourself enables you to identify what it is that is causing your stress.

When you answer these questions honestly, then you have set yourself up to understand what it is you can do. Perhaps it's just a matter of being more prepared for a job interview. It could also equate to you studying harder for an exam.

Hence, you eliminate the supposed thoughts that cause you stress. Stress and anxiety are only created by what you know. Stress cannot be created when you know that you are free. Uncertainty does not create stress but the nagging thoughts of supposition.

Once you realize that you don't know which outcome is better or worse, once you understand that uncertainty is a given, you allow yourself to be free of the stress and anxiety that is paving the way for you to do what is rightful. Knowing that uncertainty is evident, gives you the tools to prepare and look inward. Realizing that uncertainty will always be present allows us to put the best versions of ourselves into action.

If you come to realize the idea that good or bad could happen given a particular scenario (and be inventive with the scenarios) and give logical answers to these supposed bad outcomes, you will be able to understand that there are so many possible outcomes.

Take, for example, a person who feels unrecognized by their boss. One person may not find your worth in what you do, but other people find you to be indispensable. Take a bad break up. Say you got hurt from a bad split but this separation paved the way for perhaps a new and more fulfilling relationship with another person or maybe you discover that you are presently better off without the taxing relationship that ended. In other words, mindset is vital to managing stress.

We have been "programmed" by the demands of society to work under stressful conditions. Preparing for a test, or a job interview, submitting a report are just some realities we all experience. We don't know any other way of operating unless it's under circumstances of pressure and demand. Operating under pressure and fear (of rejection or reprimand) as the way to getting approval or success has been the norm for many of us.

When you are stressed while doing something, there is no fun or pleasure in the task at hand. You may procrastinate and put it off till the last minute because it does not give you the uplift of doing something you enjoy. Procrastinating only heightens the stress factor because, now, you're on limited time.

On the other hand, if what you were doing gave you pleasure, if you enjoy what you do, you would spend more time on this task, and it wouldn't bother you one bit. You look forward to doing it, and you carry out the task the best way possible because there is no accompanying stress to what needs to be done.

It is easier to be focused and creative when we are free from stress and anxiety. When we are free from stress, we can be more comfortable and authentic. Identify the source of stress. Eliminate stressors by asking yourself logical questions about the root of the stress and answer them just as honestly.

Stress makes us unhappy. It prevents us from being accessible to people. Stressed people are not pleasant to be around, and this is manifested through the interaction between people. So this is another vicious cycle in which we are trapped by the grips of stress. How you may ask? Through isolation; when we are not pleasant to be around, our response (under stress) is to withdraw. We isolate ourselves from the company of others, thereby giving more way to the stress of insecurity. This becomes a lonely cycle unless we recognize and break the cycle! When you are not stressed and happy, you are better primed to help you get what you want.

CHAPTER 8:

Loving a Person with Anxiety

Anxiety comes in many forms, and there is no magic pill that can help. Anxiety is also an individual experience that can differ in many ways. The list of things we can do to help our partner when they are having an anxiety attack differs from person to person. You should know how to recognize the symptoms and learn how to neutralize an anxiety attack by relying on previous experience.

Your involvement in your partner's journey of learning how to live a life free of anxiety is of great importance. When it comes to sudden panic attacks, you can do several things to help distract your partner and ease any suffering. When it comes to chronic anxiety, you are the one who will get involved in exposure therapy. There are specific strategies you can take into consideration when it comes to each type of anxiety.

Obsessive-Compulsive Disorder

When it comes to OCD, what you can do for your partner is not to engage in his behaviors. Also, encourage him not to give in and repeat their compulsive behaviors. If you give in and comply with your partner's OCD, you will not be helping. Although it will surely elevate the tension made by your partner's OCD, complying will reinforce the fears. For example, if your partner asks you to go to the kitchen and make sure all appliances are off, you shouldn't comply. But you should also not argue or call your partner irrational. It is ineffective, and it will only deepen the anxiety.

Discuss with your partner how is it best to approach anxiety and agree on a strategy. This is where a professional therapist will be of most use to both of you. A professional can guide you through this conversation and help both of you feel comfortable discussing the delicate topic of your partner's disorder.

You will need to learn how to change from saying things like:

"I will not go to the kitchen again, you are imagining things, and being irrational" to "I appreciate your concern about the kitchen appliances, but we agreed that the best thing we can do is to help you learn how to manage the feelings you are having right now."

Your partner will agree for their benefit that the best thing you could do is stay by their side, not check the kitchen, and help them work through the anxiety. This can be done with breathing exercises that will help your partner calm down. In time, your partner will show less fear. The OCD will decrease, and you will feel less frustrated.

CHAPTER 9:

Fear of Abandonment

A fear of abandonment is a complex phenomenon in psychology that is believed to originate from childhood loss or injury. This worry has been examined from a variety of perspectives. Concepts behind why anxiety of abandonment occurs to consist of disturbances in the regular advancement of little ones' social and mental capacities, past connections and life experiences, and direct exposure to certain norms and also concepts have been studied.

Although it is not the main phobia, the fear of desertion is probably among the most common and most damaging worries of all. Individuals with the fear of abandonment might tend to display necessary actions and also thought patterns that affect their connections, inevitably leading to the abandonment they dread becoming a reality. This anxiety can be ravaging. Recognizing this worry is the very first step towards solving it.

The worry of abandonment is the frustrating worry that individuals close to you will undoubtedly leave. Anyone can create anxiety of abandonment. It can be deeply rooted in a stressful experience you had as a youngster or a stressful relationship in the adult years. If you fear desertion, it can be virtually difficult to keep healthy and balanced relationships. This incapacitating concern can lead you to wall surface yourself off to prevent getting hurt. Or you may be unintentionally undermining partnerships.

The first step in dealing with your anxiety is to recognize why you feel in this manner. You should be able to resolve your issues and problems on your own or with treatment.

But the fears of desertion may additionally be part of a personality disorder that requires treatment. Continue the analysis to explore the reasons and also long-lasting effects of a worry of abandonment, even when you ought to seek assistance.

Signs of a Fear of Abandonment

Numerous people have a problem with anxiety. Nearly 10% of individuals in the U.S. have some type of phobia. When it involves connections, its resulting habits consist of:

- You are fast to affix, also to not available partners or relationships.
- You are reluctant to commit fully, as well as have had very few long-lasting partnerships.
- You aim to please. For some ladies, a study has also located an increase in the desire to have undesirable sex.
- As soon as in a partnership, you stay, despite how undesirable the relationship is.

- You are often hard to please as well as nitpicky.
- Emotional affection is hard for you.
- You feel insecure and unworthy of love.
- You locate it tough to rely on individuals.
- Being jealous of everybody you satisfy is not an odd sensation to you.
- Feelings of separation anxiousness are extreme.
- Feelings of underlying stress and anxiety and also clinical depression are very common to you.
- You often tend to overthink points and also work hard to identify the concealed significance in everything.
- You are hypersensitive to objections.
- You have quenched anger and also control issues.
- Self-blame prevails for you.

Sorts of Concerns of Abandonment

You may be afraid that someone you like is going to leave and not come back physically. You may fear that a person will undoubtedly desert your psychological requirements, either can hold you in relationships with moms and dad, a partner, or a good friend.

Fear of Psychological Desertion

It may be less apparent than physical truancy. However, it's no less stressful. We all have psychological needs.

When those demands aren't fulfilled, you may feel unappreciated, hated, as well as separated. You can feel quite alone, even when you remain in connection with somebody existing. If you've experienced psychological desertion in the past, primarily as a youngster, you may reside in continuous fear that it will certainly take place once more.

The Anxiety of Abandonment in Children

It's regular for babies as well as toddlers to experience a separation anxiousness phase.

They may sob, howl, or refuse to allow when a parent or critical caregiver needs to leave. Children have a hard time understanding when or if that person will certainly return. As they begin to understand that enjoyed ones do return, they outgrow their anxiety. For a lot of kids, this takes place by their third birthday celebration.

Desertion Anxiousness in Partnerships

You may be frightened to let yourself be susceptible to a company. You may have depended on issues as well as stress excessively regarding your relationship. That can make you suspicious. In time, your anxiousness can cause various other people to drawback, bolstering the cycle.

Signs and Symptoms of Fear of Abandonment

If you fear desertion, you may recognize a few of these signs and also indications:

- Overly conscious criticism

- Problem trusting in others
- Trouble making friends unless you can be confident they like you
- Taking severe procedures to avoid being rejected or separation
- A pattern of unhealthy connections
- Problem dedicating to a relationship
- Functioning hard to please the other individual as well
- Blaming yourself when things do not exercise
- Remaining in a connection even if it's not healthy and balanced for you

Abandonment Problems in Relationships

If you fear desertion in your present partnership, it might result from having been physically or emotionally abandoned in the past. For example:

- As a teen, you may have experienced the fatality or desertion of a parent or caretaker.
- You might have experienced parental forget.
- You might have been turned down by your peers.
- You experienced a prolonged health problem of an enjoyed one.
- A charming partner might have left you instantly or behaved in an undependable fashion.

Such occasions can result in a fear of desertion.

CHAPTER 10:

Toxic Relationships

Anxiety isn't always the element that affects a relationship. Sometimes it's the other way around, and the reason you have anxiety is that it is a toxic relationship. But what exactly does toxic mean? We refer to a relationship as toxic when it isn't beneficial to you and it's harmful in some way. The building blocks for a healthy relationship are made from mutual respect and admiration, but sometimes it just isn't enough.

However, there is a difference between a problematic relationship and a toxic one, and that is mainly the noxious atmosphere that surrounds you. This kind of relationship can suffocate you with time and prevent you from living a happy, productive life. Many factors lead to toxicity. It is most often caused by friction that can occur between two people that are opposites of each other. In others, nothing specific is to blame, and the toxic relationship grows from the lack of communication, the establishment of boundaries, and the ability to agree on something, or at the very least, compromise.

Take note that not all toxic relationships develop because of the couple. Sometimes there is an outlier seeking to influence conflict because they will benefit from it in some way. This type of individual preys on other people's insecurities, weaknesses, or manipulates his way inside a relationship from which he has something to gain. In some cases, a toxic person seeks to destroy a relationship to get closer to one of them. He or she may not even be aware of their damaging behavior because of a self-obsessed focus that does not extend to anyone else. Personal needs, emotions, and goals take priority over anyone else's wellbeing.

With that in mind, let's briefly explore the characteristics of a toxic relationship:

1. Poisonous: A relationship that is extremely unpleasant to be around as it poisons the surrounding environment. It makes anyone around the couple anxious, and it can even lead to psychological and emotional problems such as anxiety and depression.
2. Deadly: Toxic relationships are bad for your health. In many cases, it involves risky, destructive, and abusive behaviors. Some people end up harming themselves with alcohol, drugs, or worse. Injuries and even death can become the final result.
3. Negative: In this kind of relationship, negativity is the norm. There is no positive reinforcement, even when children are involved. The overwhelming lack of approval and emotional support is standard.
4. Harmful: Toxic relationships lack balance and awareness. Those involved are never truly aware of each other and lack the most positive principles that a healthy relationship needs. Toxicity

also promotes immoral and malicious acts that harm a romantic relationship.

While it is true that some of them are, that's not always the case. However, psychopaths are expert manipulators due to their ability to mask their true feelings and intentions. These people have a psychological disorder that makes their personalities imposing, pretentious, and even impulsive. Many aren't aware of their behavior and the effects it has on others. They tend to be self-absorbed and expect a great deal from others while being narcissistic and deceitful. In other words, they lack insight as well as empathy. Psychopaths are people who seek attention, admiration, and acceptance, but they will need to accept their responsibilities and the needs of others.

Why and how would anyone end up in a relationship with someone who displays psychopathic traits? The answer lies in their ability to maintain appearances and manipulate others. If they realize you see through their charade, they will do anything to convince you that they are a good person. They may start doing good deeds, not out of empathy and love, but out of the need to redeem themselves. In many cases, these people can recover if their psychopathic disorder isn't too severe. With help, they can gain control over themselves and their toxic behavior, so they can live a productive life without hurting others in the process.

As mentioned earlier, toxic relationships don't always involve psychopaths or those who display similar traits. In many situations, these relationships are the way they are due to decent people that are terrible decision-makers or lack social skills. Taking a wrong turn in life happens to everyone, and many people change but not always for the better.

Warning Signs

Now that you can better identify toxic relationships and the kind of people that are involved let's see if you're in one or not. Some underlying issues and disorders can make people behave negatively. However, they can still be excellent partners. With that said, here's a list of questions you can ask yourself to learn more about your relationship:

1. How do you feel in the company of your partner?
2. Do you feel happy, safe, and nurtured in the presence of your significant other?
3. Are all the other people involved in your relationship safe and happy? For instance your children (if you have any), parents, and friends, and so on. As mentioned earlier, people tend to avoid toxic relationships instead of being in contact with them.
4. Do you experience anxiety or panic attacks when you are about to discuss something with your partner?
5. Can you think of any scenarios in which you were manipulated to do something that wasn't for your best interest?
6. Is your partner pushing the limits of what you would consider ethical? Is he or she even crossing the line of what is legal?
7. Does your partner push you to perform challenging tasks that you consider entirely unnecessary? These challenges may seem

pointless, and that you need to resolve them just because it's what your partner wants.

8. Do you feel emotionally strained and exhausted after interacting with your partner?

If you can answer a few of these questions, you are likely in a toxic relationship that may be making you anxious and damaging your health. You then need to decide for yourself whether you wish to stay in this kind of relationship to repair it or leave. If you do decide to stay, you need to make some decisions. For instance, you need to feel in control with the idea of resisting all the negativity that comes with a toxic partner, because you will need to endure feelings of anxiety and stress. You need to ask yourself whether you are gaining enough from that relationship and whether it's worth sacrificing yourself for it.

Handling a Toxic Relationship

As mentioned, a toxic relationship can be a powerful source of anxiety. It doesn't have to be a romantic relationship either. Some of them you can avoid by cutting contact with some people to feel relief. However, there are certain people you simply cannot break away from, whether they are romantic partners or your mother-in-law.

The first step is to accept the inescapable situation. When your options are limited, you cannot achieve relief by avoidance, and acceptance leads to a decrease in anxiety. You may be tempted to be hostile towards that person, but it won't help. Instead, it will just add to your worries and stress. At this point, your only alternative is managing your anxiety by admitting to yourself that you may never be able to get along with that person. Also, you can attempt to ignore him or her completely by never going to spend time together and ignoring any contact. However, none of these tactics usually work. Resistance can help in the short term, but it will continue generating anxiety and stress because the toxic person knows how to get under your skin and take advantage of you. Accept that this relationship is difficult and challenges you, but you are doing your best to make it better. That doesn't mean you should completely surrender. By accepting your situation, you will allow yourself new possibilities and new options instead of repeatedly punishing yourself.

Take note that for the process of acceptance to take hold, you need to be consciously aware that you are not responsible for anyone else's emotions and reactions. Toxic behavior often makes people blame you for their situation and feelings. Do not accept any of that, as you are not the reason for their suffering. They need to take responsibility for their thoughts and actions instead of blaming others. The second step is telling the truth. If a toxic relationship is creating stress, likely, you often lie to avoid conflict, which causes even more anxiety. The problem is that when you lie to such a person, you enable them and become partially responsible for the reality they create, leading to the toxic environment surrounding them. For instance, let's say you intentionally didn't invite the problematic person to your birthday. When confronted about it, you may be tempted to say that you sent an invitation but used the wrong address, or it went into the spam folder. Lying isn't easy, especially if you are an anxious person. People can tell, especially if you tend to make excuses for yourself often enough. Instead of lying, you should tell the truth and the real truth. This means that you shouldn't use an excuse. Just say they make you uncomfortable and extremely anxious, that is why you didn't invite them. Telling the truth can be difficult and even painful because it affects others. It takes a great deal of courage and once you get through the experience, you will feel a powerful sense of relief. In the end, it's better to get something off your chest instead of carrying it.

CHAPTER 11:

The Diamond Inside of Anxiety

To the vast majority, fear strikes like power from the depths and draws them into an infernal world in a blast of panic from their highly functioning everyday lives. Where they were once excited to move into a healthy married life, now they are so concerned about it that it hampers their ability to feed, sleep and work properly, let alone to plan a wedding. You would like the anxiety to disappear, thinking incorrectly that it is an indication that you are in the wrong relationship and that the only solution is to leave. That's when they find their way to Google's "engagement anxiety" or "marriage terror."

It is a challenge to make; nobody would want to live with the demon of fear, so you should understand why you want the demon to vanish. Yet there can be no real healing without the ability to discover its origins and heights.

It is a strange and counterintuitive assertion, but what all my clients realize eventually is that the fear-based thoughts and repetitive questions contain great information. This will help you reach this knowledge by dressing like a hero or heroine embarking into what Joseph Campbell calls the "Hero's Journey." Then you can have the ability to dive into your psyche's darkest areas and keep a light of reality about what you are seeking in them. And here's a nugget of confidence to combat the fear of looking inside. There is an unharmed warehouse of sadness, a soft space of vulnerability, a shy person, a river of terror, a warehouse of myths about love, marriage, romanticism, and intimacy. And when you learn to take care of your difficult feelings and to substitute false assumptions with the truth, you will find a degree of harmony, confidence, and healing, which you had never learned. The uncertainty you feel about your relationship is not new, and you have not felt insecure in your life for the first time. If you, like most people who find me, have frequently or continuously suffered from anxiety throughout your life, now is your chance to repair it.

The magic of this deep soul research shows what the soul is trying to express. The soul wants wholeness, peace, and serenity, but it does not always know how to fulfill these wants. Instead of specifically requesting more life, for instance, we prefer to project the will into our partner in the form: "He's not interesting enough." If we stick to that concept and assume it's real, we lose the chance to mine for the diamond within anxiety.

I've always told you that the purpose of concentrating on the negative attributes of our partners is to shield or protect yourself from the hard feelings caused by transitions: the remorse of letting go and the dream of the ideal mate, the uncertainty of jumping into the unknown, and the insecurity accompanying the danger of love. But I realized recently that, while the thoughts defend against painful feelings, they are also gates to expand our consciousness and to deepen our emotional and spiritual development.

To break through the nervous barrier and hit the inside gem. It is important to understand which questions lead to diamonds. I have grouped the most common issues according to their positive role to promote this process.

Finding Your Way through the 'Mirror Maze' of Emotions and Relationships

It may also feel like a day-to-day life for those with shyness and anxiety. If you are an insecure or shy guy (or woman), you probably have smart, talented, funny, affectionate, and interesting friends, but you are still so unsure about yourself that you are lost in trying to find out who you should be rather than who you are. You think your true self is "too isolated" from those around you. And when you care about others, lead and take responsibility, you doubt your worth and how you make a difference for others. You certainly have worked hard to be a member of the community or, more frequently, to avoid being insulted by a lack of attributes that will make you attractive or appealing to others.

You may be married or have relationships and are involved in caring for others, but you feel you've never been able to express your thoughts, emotions, dreams, and interests directly. You could doubt whether anyone would hear or care, even if you spoke out. Your days and hours are full of tasks and events, but despite what you are doing, you find very little satisfaction.

Relations and social interactions can be a labyrinth of reflections and dead ends to us, shy men, like this hall of mirrors. When you obey one rule, you will never know how to find your way out, keep your eyes on your feet, and know where you are. You will concentrate on placing every foot carefully before you if you are not disturbed by flashing lights, changing colors, and tenting views of the exit. You can check your way and move forward with each stage.

Fear and anxiety work best when disturbed and unsure. The confounding wind of interactions, talk, and movement around you may become daunting if you feel that you are responsible for following these sometimes-conflicting currents and reacting to them. When you concentrate on knowing yourself and being attentive to yourself, your values, perceptions, emotions, and awareness, you can start the journey out of the stormy labyrinth.

Money and Finance: The Cause of Anxieties for Most Families

Martha had a night of restlessness. The next day she got a credit card company billing statement telling her she was behind schedule on her monthly charge. Each time a debt collector called her at the office and home, at times, even in odd hours of the night, she always felt threatened. They have had trouble paying the mortgage and the monthly rates for the new vehicle. Their financial struggles are partially due to her husband Ben, who admits himself to be a major donor. Ben is a passionate driver who invests a great deal of time, "spicing up" his Japanese car and making it look like the street racer in the movie "Too

Hard, Too Furious." Both Ben and Martha have been subjected to tremendous stress and anxiety each day. Despite their financial problems, they are struggling a lot and sharing the blame for slipping into the debt pit. It is not shocking that money is now a big cause of divorce.

Money or, better, lack of money is one of the key causes of marriage tension and anxiety. In the United States, the average household has a credit card debt of at least $9,200. Bens and Martha have no experience in financial growth methods and techniques. The common mistake hard-pressed couples make is that they invest more than they can return.

We are all faced with various obstacles and money pressures. Facing these financial challenges can be very daunting if nothing is done about them early. Owing to the relentless demand for our everyday living, it is also the leading cause of stress and anxiety that can destroy your mental and physical well-being.

However, money should help us better our condition and not make our lives miserable. To raising the burden created by financial difficulties, the following financial management advice should be read and taken into consideration: First, create a practical budget. It is the very first step to gaining control of your finances. Create a list of all the money or bills you have to pay. Then choose to pay them one by one based on your fixed payment power. It is also important to mention all other revenue sources. The next move is for all of your "fixed" expenses such as mortgages, rent, car payments, fuel, credit card, and insurance premiums to be written down. Then calculate how much money you have left to know exactly what you spent on other things. Before you finish paying for priority accounts, it is necessary to adhere to your payment schedule and not build any other payable. You can track where your money goes with a small notebook. Moreover, using a budgeting system for your computer can be a helpful method to manage your checkbook.

The second step is to teach your children money. Children are now easily tempted by advertisements and marketing gimmicks. With peer pressure and the relentless blockade of fads, children can lose their interest in something they don't need. They have to be told how difficult it is to raise money, and that they cannot purchase anything they see in a toy store, on TV. Children about eight years of age can already be taught to handle and start saving allowances.

Another step in the direction of financial freedom, whether you believe it or not, is to contact your creditors. Explain your condition and ask them to reorganize your loans. Ask them to offer a debt reduction solution but ensure that interest rates are reasonable and regular payments can be made. Seek to persuade the creditors to build a new payment plan, which would lead to a win-win financial situation.

If you want to regain financial independence, cost reduction initiatives should also be an automatic undertaking. You can save money by actually doing stuff like turning off the lights if you don't need them, scheduling your journeys or grocery store orders, and only cutting back on sales of fast food. Both of these helps to reduce your monthly expenses. You might, for example, avoid subscribing to the magazine or select a cheaper cable with fewer channels.

You should consult a financial planner on investment options and securities such as bonds and inventories if you have enough savings.

CHAPTER 12:

Strategies to Improve Existing Relationships

If you've found someone you want to spend the foreseeable future with and would like to either start on the right foot or work to improve the connection you already have, consider some of the following points:

1. Have Common Visions and Values

If one person is a spendthrift and the other is thrifty if one is watching their diet and the other eats only junk food if one is on the right and the other on the left of the political spectrum, etc., chances are high that battles will take place frequently.

For your relationship to last, you must have a set of commonalities for which you come together and a vision that allows you to project yourselves into a bright future.

All of this helps to share dreams and a good understanding of each other!

2. Gratify The Other and Give Recognition

Whether you're married or not, much of what destroys couples and relationships comes from taking each other for granted. How does this translate into daily life?

When you refrain from putting in the effort, when you do not do your part to nurture the relationship, when you criticize too much and too often, when you don't take their feelings to the heart or acknowledge their struggles, and when you naively believe that your partner will love you forever, regardless of what you do.

Relationships do not work like that.

For each person in a relationship to feel loved and appreciated, both must express gratitude and recognition for the other regularly.

This attitude nurtures collaboration, encourages a strong connection, and helps us appreciate our partner. They do not owe us their affection, so knowing that it is freely given is gratifying.

3. Be Proud of The Person With Whom You Are In a Relationship

How can you live happily as a couple if you do not admire, at the very least, the person you are with?

There's no need to have received a Nobel Prize, cured cancer, or solved world hunger. If you do not appreciate at least one trait of the other person (intelligence, beauty, determination, courage, humor), you do not appreciate their place in your life. People gravitate towards those who express love, acceptance, and fulfillment. Make your partner feel loved and accepted all the time.

4. Have Realistic Expectations

Some women are continually looking for an impossible Prince Charming and believe that love must resemble a fairy tale, while men may be influenced by the unreasonable standards set by the media.

Whatever these unfounded expectations are, if they are unrealistic, by definition, they will generate disappointment.

Research into positive psychology has shown that it is better to have realistic and modest expectations as much as possible, even in your relationships.

If you are happy with what you have, you will find satisfaction.

If you are always looking to replace your partner with someone "better," without seeing their true qualities, you will condemn yourself to an eternal search for an illusion that exists only in your imagination.

5. Give Regular and Ample Affection

Research has also shown that long-lasting couples are those who have been able to gradually replace love and passion with attachment.

We are not aware of it, but a lot of our behavior is determined by our hormones and our neurotransmitters. Cuddling, affection, and tenderness stimulate the production of oxytocin, the hormone of attachment.

If you want to feed the well-being of your partner, you must not forget the power of showing affection.

6. Do Not Let The Sexual Flame Go Out

After the passion at the beginning of your relationship, as time goes on, the frequency at which you make love might reduce. This can be for many reasons, none of which should be used to assign blame.

If this tendency continues, sexual desire may end up being extinguished. Without (necessarily) bringing out the whip and the handcuffs, it is possible to continue to spark the sexual flame.

Yes, some clothes and toys can help, but the real key is to devote enough time to intimacy in your relationship, despite the tumult of everyday life.

Eating well, exercising, and staying healthy can help keep the flame alive despite the passage of time. But, it also depends on your taste and your partner's. This fits into a more general vision which also comes from your personal development and health.

7. Be Open To Improving and Working On Yourself

If you or your partner constantly live in a state of pride and self-denial, it is clear that the relationship is preparing for doom.

Being in a partnership or relationship means working on yourself, making compromises, acknowledging shortcomings and mistakes, and working to correct them.

Proud people usually avoid this subject carefully: themselves, and more particularly their mistakes and faults. It will be difficult for you to live with such a person unless you dream of sharing your life with a manipulator.

8. Stay Faithful

To be faithful implies getting out of the excessive egotism that makes us prioritize our pleasure while ignoring that of the person we love.

A minimally empathetic person will quickly realize that if they would not want the other person to cheat on them, it is not acceptable behavior for themselves either.

If you claim to love the other person, deceiving them becomes the last thing on your mind.

Love is one of the richest experiences we have to live by through happiness and hardship. Why sully that with lies and unfaithfulness?

In short, romantic relationships are dynamic, like life, like those who live them. To live these enriching relationships, you must first come to recognize that your point of view is not the only point of view.

Only by trying to understand others do you come to build more fruitful relationships.

Respect, empathy and communication lead to more satisfying partnerships than the need to constantly be right.

Conflicts cannot be avoided in relationships. Two people who bring different life experiences to the table will inevitably have disagreements.

But when you strive to achieve your goals regardless of what the other person wants, you engage in behaviors that can only lead to a break-up. The challenge may be to bring different motivations together through common values, but you have a big tool to meet this challenge: communication.

To share your life with another person, basic wisdom requires you to make some sacrifices. When you do not communicate with your partner, even if the goal is to avoid conflict at all costs, you will only achieve even more disastrous results.

Regardless of whether you've been dating your partner for a short or long time, strong connections are formed when you accept the responsibility of making an effort and considering your partner's point of view.

While each relationship is unique, no relationship is impeccable. By doing these 9 things to improve your bond, you won't just guarantee a quality connection with your partner, you'll also demonstrate that you're resolved to work for one.

1. Ask Your Partner Something New

Communication is the measure of togetherness in a relationship. It's pleasant to ask how your partner's day went, yet it's exhausting when you ask again and again. Communication must not be boring or redundant, so it is your joint responsibility to keep yourself engaged with dialogues that are engaging and meaningful at the same time.

2. Assign A Month To Month Night Out On The Town

Despite your busy schedules, ensure that you plan a night when the two of you will spend time together. Be consistent and be devoted to it once you have agreed on a date with your partner. If you're hoping to zest up your relationship or want to try something other than Netflix, leaving the house is a far more promising endeavor. More memories are made out in the world than on your couch.

3. Express Your Appreciation

The solace that a relationship offers is the reason we will, in general, ignore what our partner does and treat their demonstrations of affection as mandatory. To put it truly, your partner doesn't need to fill your gas tank or purchase your preferred frozen yogurt. They decide to because they love you, and your recognition and appreciation of the gesture will strengthen your relationship and inspire your partner to continue to be attentive and make you feel appreciated.

4. Change Your Timetable

We know you're autonomous and don't anticipate ceasing your life for anybody (and you shouldn't need to). Even though you have different responsibilities outside of your relationship, it's a nice thought to check your calendars and see if conflicts are preventing you from spending time together.

5. Keep In Mind The Little Things

Another approach to add importance to your discussion is to genuinely tune in to what your loved one is saying and talk about it later on. If you need to, make note of something you talked about that you want to remember, or an event your partner mentioned that you want to follow up on. It's often the little things in conversations and relationships that make the biggest difference. Also keep in mind that everyday things, while being small, can contribute to the happiness in your relationship. Reminders that you love the other person, have listened to them, or are thinking about them all seem like small gestures, but they are powerful.

6. Demonstrate Your Love

Apart from appreciating your partner, you need to let them know the extent of your love for them. You express your love through different gestures, from holding your partner's hand at a café to hitting the hay together toward the night's end. These gestures do not only show how you feel about your partner, but they also indicate that you are proud and appreciative of them.

7. Get Familiar With Your Partner's Behavior

Does your partner wish to be left alone when they are vexed? How do they react in some specific situations? These inquiries are basic, however, the responses to them will enable you to comprehend the behavior of your partner and prevent you from offending them accidentally. The way your partner views the world is not the same way you do, so the way they act in situations will most likely differ as well.

8. Learn When To Apologize

You need to realize that being correct isn't as significant as being empathetic. Though clashes occur in a relationship, few arguments are a test that should be won. What I am trying to pass across is simple: know what is worth fighting for and when you need to accept the blame. It is better to say sorry than turn a small argument into a relationship-breaking crisis.

Conclusion

Anxiety can feel like an additional individual in the relationship, an irritating element that pushes among you and your accomplice. The tension appears to perpetuate uncertainty and disarray in the relationship continually. Regardless of whether you are telling your accomplice that you experience the ill effects of nervousness, or getting some information about their tension, how the subject is examined can represent the moment of truth in a relationship. Individuals who experience the ill effects of nervousness invested a great deal of their energy stressing and envisioning situations in which everything without exception could turn out badly.

They over examine their connections, posing negative inquiries, and enabling the responses to reflect terrible results. While it is typical for individuals to have these sorts of considerations and questions now and again, nervousness intensifies them. Those with a tension issue consider these inquiries regularly and with power. Individuals with anxiety envision the direst outcome imaginable, enabling their psyches to assume control over their sound point of view. Musings cause physiological manifestations in the body. Uneasiness doesn't just influence the individual experiencing it. It can put anxiety on your accomplice and can pulverize a relationship.

Tension doesn't have to risk your relationship. At the point when you overcome your feelings and utilize the correct adapting systems, you can have a healthy relationship. These adapting systems will prevent uneasiness from also causing anxiety in your relationship. The duty regarding assuming responsibility for your feelings lies with you as the sufferer of uneasiness. You are seeing a specialist who can show you solid methods for dealing with stress that will improve your satisfaction in and outside of your relationship. If you are in a long-haul submitted relationship, you may consider heading off to a few couple's sessions to work through any nervousness that is present in your relationship. By doing this, you are easing the heat off of your accomplice and your relationship.

At the point when you have negative musings, anxiety takes steps to crush you and makes them cry that your life is loaded with misfortune. Be that as it may, the fact of the matter is your very own negative musings make you the cause of all your problems. At the point when you enable yourself to enjoy negative thoughts, you are making your misfortune. You have to turn out to be increasingly mindful again and hear the words as you express them to yourself to sift through the pessimism. When you can perceive the negative words and thoughts, you can stop and counter them with positive or elective messages. By being certain and hopeful, you can transform antagonism into truth, not fear.

Because things haven't turned out in different connections or you have been frustrated in the past doesn't imply that they won't be diverse this time. Pessimism doesn't need to be something you are tormented with until the end of time. You are the ace of your destiny, and when you change pessimism to energy, all of you, your hopeful standpoint radiates through your relationship.

Another issue that stems from low confidence and nervousness is desire. Desire can assume control over your life if you don't take a few to get back some composure on it and it can overwhelm you, it can be a terrifying feeling to feel. It can frequently destroy connections and propagate a negative idea. At the point when you enable envy to overwhelm you or to shape how you think about yourself or your accomplice, you are conceivably disrupting your relationship. By attempting to comprehend where your envious sentiments are originating from, figuring out how to manage them, and discovering approaches to adjust to your feelings, you are allowing your relationship to thrive. The individuals who experience the ill effects of uneasiness know about these dangerous musings experiencing your psyche, yet envy starts to frame when these thoughts begin to get fanatical.

The main problem comes in when those with uneasiness will, in general, retreat trying to shield themselves from the envisioned risk or torment that they believe is happening. Be that as it may, the more you retreat, the more removed your accomplice will become, and the more envious you will turn. By effectively chipping away at your nervousness and your jealous sentiments, you are making your relationship a need and deciding to love and close with your accomplice rather than desirous and unreliable. At the point when you choose to battle desire, you are intentionally telling your accomplice that you have a sense of security and are secure enough in yourself and them to place your trust in your relationship.

The most well-known indications of a relationship in a difficult situation are how the accomplices differ or battle with one another and how they settle the contention between them. Their goals, whether negative or positive, can influence the tone of the relationship and how clashes are taken care of later on. Contradictions that form into petty squabbling or on edge consistent clashes, as a rule, end up in a more uncertain possibility of the relationship enduring. Fortunately, there are arrangements, and settling strife can be moderately simple with the assistance of a specialist. If that you and your accomplice are not yet capable and the purpose of seeing a therapist, rehearsing sympathy without judgment will go far in settling strife. Sympathetic tuning in and proclamations should be possible by telling your accomplice that you are tuning in. Since as individuals, they experience the ill effects of tension that are commonly centered on themselves, they will, in general, contend such that it makes them like themselves. At the point when individuals practice compassionate tuning in and correspondence, they guarantee that their accomplice realizes that they are being tuned in to. Fortunately, it gets considerably more straightforward.

While building a compassionate proclamation, one should utilize, "So you feel that…." This maintains the emphasis on your accomplice and away from your sentiments of uneasiness. At the point when the two accomplices utilize this system to listen cautiously to the passionate needs of their life partner, it stays away from strife and addresses the more profound issues close by.

A specific degree of anxiety is something to be thankful for and inquire about and shows that great pressure can inspire and energize an individual in their lives. Nervousness can be only the admonition sign. You have to carry attention to your present circumstance and roll out some important improvements throughout your life. Consistent stress and anxiety can be a sign that a few parts of your life are off track and need altering. Even though your nervousness indications can be hard to oversee, by setting aside some effort to investigate and taking a shot at adapting to your uneasiness, it very well may be a genuine open door for self-development. Whenever tension strikes, think about what message it has for you and the potential changes you may need to make in your life. As opposed to continually being viewed as an obstruction, tension may assist you with feeling progressively inspired and arranged when looked at with difficulties.

Anxiety doesn't have to control your life or wreck your relationship. It very well may be utilized to fabricate a solid character and help with building up an impressive, regarded character. A solid character doesn't mean you should be boisterous, scary, or over the top to show your character. It is conceivable to have a solid character in calm certainty too. Uneasiness has its favorable circumstances. It sends a sign to the body that something is significant or could represent a peril to you. Having uneasiness about your accomplice shoes that you care for them on a more profound level, if you didn't encounter nervousness, you would most likely, at some point or another, find that you couldn't care less for your accomplice.

Intense tension should be abolished, however, particularly if you will probably push ahead into an important association with your accomplice. Although nervousness can't be relieved, it unquestionably can be controlled, and you as the sufferer of tension have a decision in whether you decide to participate in your very own negative conduct. Nervousness builds inspiration, reason, and satisfaction to a certain degree. Truly, we concur that it can feel dreadful, yet outfit effectively, nervousness can feature regions in our lives that we have to investigate. It urges us to roll out the improvements we have to make to carry on with a more joyful, increasingly happy life.

Take control of your anxiety today. Build a more grounded relationship and be a superior you!

Lightning Source UK Ltd.
Milton Keynes UK
UKHW021846220221
379219UK00004B/585

9 781801 764988